Fresh Expressions

An Introduction to the use of the
European Principles of Design

BY KATHRYN BARKER NDSF FSF

PREFACE

This book is intended to be a simplified introduction to the use of European Principles and Elements of Design approached from a uniquely British perspective.

I initially started to write this as a guide for Level 3 Floristry students who would be at a stage where more modern design work was being attempted and an understanding of the background of the Design Principles is therefore required in order to go forward. However, appreciation of these Design Principles is applicable to a far greater audience of florists, flower arrangers and hobbyists and so I have prepared this work with such people in mind.

I believe it is vitally important that we, as 'British' florists use these Principles of Design as an aid in our quest to create beautiful floristry.

We have our traditional designs based on the 2/3rds to 1/3rd proportions and the time has now come for us to move on, whilst at the same time retaining the elements that make us quintessentially English.

Each and every country that makes use of these Principles of Design to create their floral arrangements has their own identity and style. It is vital that British florists do not adopt any one particular country's style. We need to find our own style and interpretation. We need to discover a balance between all of the other styles and interpretations and decide which elements suit us best as a body of British florists.

I hope that this introduction has helped to remove any of the confusion, so that you can begin to create beautiful floristry designs in a more natural way.

Within this work I have limited myself to an explanation of the basic Principles and Elements of Design. There is much more to explore and experience and, as you become fluent in the use of these basic Principles, I am certain that your floristry designs will advance and you will then delve deeper and further this knowledge.

I hope you will enjoy reading - and then practicing - the Principles I have presented within this book.

Kathryn Barker NDSF FSF

CONTENTS

1 IN THE BEGINNING

In the beginning were the Ancient Greeks, in particular, one Greek man, named Pythagoras.

Being of a precise and methodical mind he developed a mathematical equation to explain the basis for designs throughout nature and life in general. He believed that everything could be explained by a mathematical concept.

'Phi' is this concept and it is the mathematical principle or equation developed, or at least, discovered, by Pythagoras in 600BC. The value of Phi has been calculated to be 1.618.

This is not intended to be a book about mathematics; however, this principle defines the concept of natural harmony and is fundamental to understanding the Principles of Design.

Pythagoras wanted to prove that it was not by chance alone that beauty could be found. Using his mathematical principle he proved that the balance between form, function and natural designs is the result of a precise mathematical relationship. The Greeks used this mathematical equation to create architectural masterpieces, such as the Parthenon, and we continue today to see examples of this within almost every trade and lifestyle.

A few years later, an Italian mathematician by the name of Leonardo Pisano (meaning Leonardo of Pisa, [1175-1250]), used Pythagoras' theory to develop a number sequence that is visually simpler and easier to understand for design purposes. Leonardo's nickname was 'Fibonacci'. This name was taken from his father's name, Bonacci. Fibonacci means 'son of Bonacci'.

There is actually some doubt as to whether Fibonacci himself developed this mathematical sequence, even though it is attributed to him, but I am not going to enter into the debate! What matters is that the simplicity and logic behind the equation has enabled us to apply this sequence in relation to floristry designs, the principle behind the definitions of our proportions and scales.

Leonardo is now known in history for the Fibonacci sequence of numbers. This is a sequence in which every number is the sum of the previous two numbers. For example:

$$1 + 2 = 3$$

$$2 + 3 = 5$$

$$3 + 5 = 8$$

So the sequence is: 1, 3, 5, 8, 13, 21, 34, 55, 89, 144, and so on.

It should come as no surprise to discover that Fibonacci used Phi as the basis for his sequences. Ever since Leonardo Pisano, we have been designing and creating buildings, sculptures and paintings that are in accord with the dimensions contained within the Fibonacci sequence. The Colosseum in Rome is a typical example.

In effect, anything that has been created using these principles is deemed to be aesthetically pleasing to the eye. This is called, among other things, 'the golden rule'. The golden rule is also often referred to as 'the divine principle' and it is perhaps this name that probably best describes how we as florists would use it. Naturally, as florists, we have introduced our own definitions and rules that we follow called the Principles and Elements of Design. Every society or craft, it seems, has to invent its own terminology to promote its own 'mysteries'. Florists appear to be no exception and we have carried on this fine tradition.

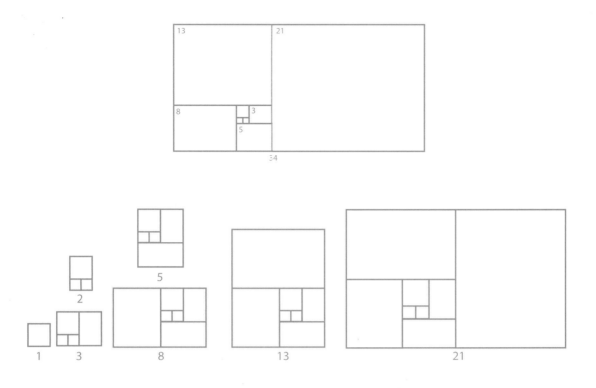

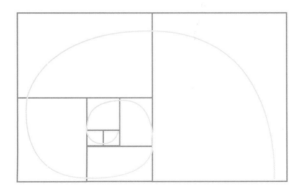

As you will see in the diagram the use of the Fibonacci number sequence creates a particular growth pattern. Look at the simplified pattern within the rectangles and you can see how the shape develops because of this sequence. Then, take a look at the spiral drawn within the squares. This mathematical spiral gives us an impression of the kind of spiral that often appears within nature.

2 NATURAL GENIUS

When you consider the patterns of growth within nature, these always appear to follow a process or pattern. This process or pattern can be explained by using Phi (Pi) and the Fibonacci numbers. Phi can be used to understand how it is that, no matter how far from the central point of growth you travel, nature is still able to get equal spacing of its parts. We do not need to explain this fully, but simply understand that there is a pattern being followed. It is enough that nature obviously understands and it has only taken mankind a few thousand years to catch up!

Look at the following photographs and try to follow the natural growth patterns and how they spiral. The growth patterns are the same as the Phi rectangle and spirals.

THE VITRUVIAN MAN

Marcus Vitruvius was a Roman Architect in 1BC. Whilst he may, at face value, seem to have nothing to do with floristry in the 21st Century, there is a link. In one of the books Marcus published, the design of buildings and temples was discussed, along with an emerging concept that man has the same symmetrical proportions as buildings! Unfortunately he left no drawings or sketches to help illustrate this principle and thus it was that a space was left in history for Leonardo da Vinci to provide the drawing of Vitruvian Man. Leonardo drew the Vitruvian Man in 1490. In fact, Leonardo da Vinci had several contemporaries, such as Fra Giovanni Giocondo, Cesare Cesariano, Francesco Giorgi and Mariano di Lacopo, who all drew their own versions of the Vitruvian Man. However, it was Leonardo's drawing that proved to be the most accurate, standing the test of time.

Marcus Vitruvius

Leonardo da Vinci

Leonardo da Vinci was born on April 15th 1452 and died in 1519. He was a famous Italian Renaissance artist, sculptor, engineer, scientist and inventor. He believed the human body to be an analogy for the workings of the universe.

So, what has this to do with floristry design?

Well, Leonardo da Vinci also used the Phi equation when he drew the famous human body diagram below. Even the miracle of the human body follows the same beauteous principles as the rest of nature. The human body follows the 3:5:8 proportions that Marcus Vitruvius, all those years before, had noticed.

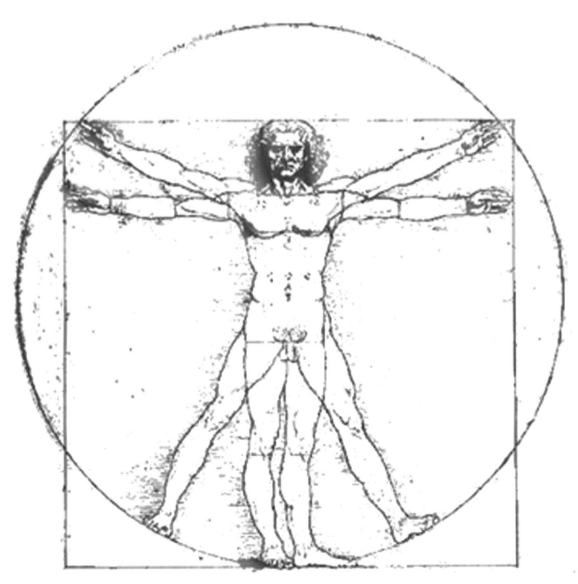

PHI PROPORTIONS IN NATURE : SUNFLOWERS

Plants have particular points of growth, which are located at the meristem. On most plants the meristem moves in relation to the light. Plants attempt to grow in such a way as to capture maximum light exposure on each leaf. In order to achieve this goal, a plant will grow its leaves within a natural spiral. This spiral can be explained using the principles of Phi. In effect, Phi ensures that, because the leaves have grown equidistant from each other, the upper leaves will not overshadow the lower ones.

Examine the leaf position of these sunflowers:

In these two photographs, the spiralling of the leaves can be easily seen. Other flowers grow their leaves and petals to the same proportions.

As well as examining the sunflower, look at the following flowers. Look at how their petals spiral around, achieving a pattern of growth that can be explained by Phi and thereby fitting into the Fibonacci number sequence.

3 FLORISTRY PRINCIPLES OF DESIGN

THE BACKGROUND TO DESIGN

Phi may be the true beginning of floristry Principles and Elements of Design, but who instigated their use in flower arrangements? How did we come to relate them to our floral designs?

I will resist the enticement of giving you a complete review of each period in English floral design! Suffice to say that floral design has naturally evolved through each and every period of history. Every period has had influential designers, who have propelled us forward into the next exciting development. We have experienced the formality of Art Deco with its geometric designs, the liberation of Art Nouveau with sensuous linear curves, Byzantine design challenged us with its stylised forms, and Baroque impressed with its decorative urns and cherubs. There have been many styles over many periods and each one has had its own individual impact on the development of floral design in this country.

Currently, we are once again heavily influenced by European designers. How we interpret and implement these new influences is something that has yet to be fully defined. It is for the current generation of British florists to determine how the new European styles will shape and influence the British designs of the future.

FIRST STEPS

There are several ways of looking at floristry designs to help us understand these new Principles of Design. However, for simplicity, let us consider the approach described below.

VISUAL DOMINANCE

The most visually dominant part of your arrangement could be '8'.
The sub-dominant part would be '5'. The least dominant part would be '3'.

At its most basic it can be illustrated as follows:

Overall shape	'8'
Flowers	'5'
Container	'3'

An alternative, and possibly more easily understood, terminology for the labelling of visual dominance can be:

Principle	(8)
Secondary	(5)
Complimentary	(3)

Illustration Number 1

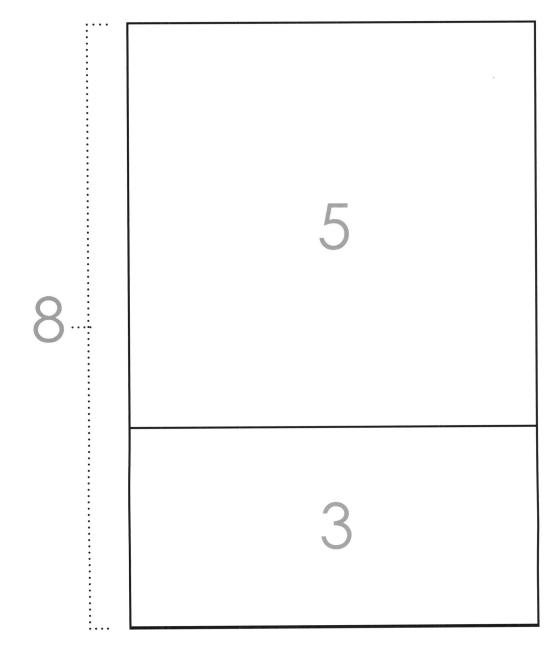

FLOWER PROPORTION

To add further interest (and risk just a little confusion!) to the design, the outline form of individual flowers would also be 3:5:8 dependent on the size.

Look at the following suggestions of flower proportions:

Gerbera	8
Rosa	5
Muscari	3

So, whilst the individual flower size is important, the actual placement of the flowers within the design can also change the proportions.

For example, one large Allium is less dominant than a placement of three large-headed Rosa blooms placed close together, even though, as an individual flower the Allium is far more substantial and dominant than the rose.

FLOWER POSITIONING

Each separate grouping of flower material would be positioned in the design at different heights: 8 - the tallest, 5 - middle placement, and 3 - the lowest placement of flowers.

Illustration Number 2

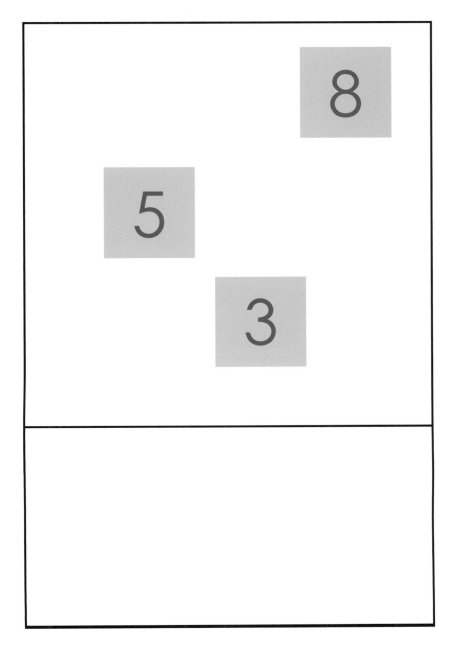

But remember that each of these 3 groups of flowers also has the flowers positioned in the 3:5:8 proportions. So, when you choose your flowers, do so with care and thought. One point to bear in mind is that the proportions and positions of the flowers can be related back to the original spiral sequence.

Illustration Number 3

NEGATIVE SPACE

Lastly, the distance or negative space between the flowers is also 3:5:8 in proportion.

Illustration Number 4

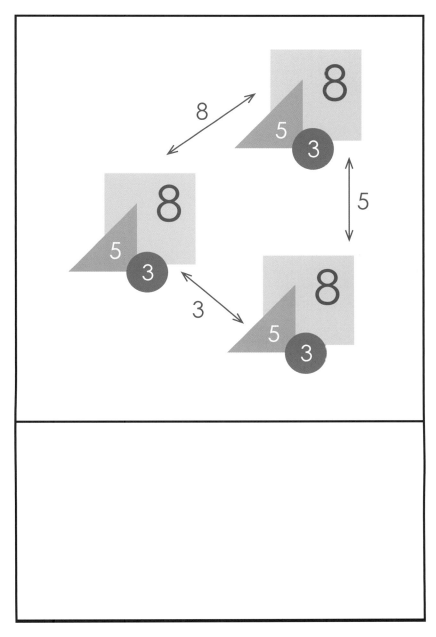

In the UK, if the outline of a floral design is Symmetrical, then our flower placements are also symmetrically and evenly positioned. If we choose to create an Asymmetrical arrangement, then the outline is asymmetrical and the flower positions follow suit.

When using the new Principles of Design we can choose to make an arrangement with an overall symmetrical outline shape, whilst placing the flowers in groups with several unevenly spaced points of growth, thereby making the flower placements asymmetrical, for example: the distance between the groups is uneven in length.

4 THE VISUAL IMPACT OF FLOWERS

Every flower provides its own unique form of visual impact: from the fluffiness of Gypsophilia, the sleek and sensual lines of the Calla lily, to the majestic structure of a hanging Heliconia. All have their own visual impact. How you choose to use the flowers depends upon the impact you wish them to have in your design.

Flowers can be placed into any 1 of 3 categories:

High Impact flowers (e.g. Heliconia, Helianthus).

Average Impact flowers (e.g. Rosa, Celosia).

Low Impact flowers (e.g. low spreading flowers, growing flat, sand/stones).

High Impact Flowers – these flowers should only be used in small quantities because their bold outline form can dominate any arrangement.

Average Impact Flowers – these flowers are your normal 'everyday' standard of flower. They are attractive in their own right but not too overwhelming in colour or form. They are best used in groups rather than individually.

Low Impact Flowers – Often known as a 'filler' flower, such as Gypsophilia. It is best used in a group, massed, as it needs very little space.

Every aspect of your floral arrangement will create its own sense of importance. It is up to you to decide each individual flower's effect within your design.

Remember not to confuse the design. Do not overuse any of the flowers, whatever their 'impact category'. Less, very definitely, is more!

FLOWER FORMS

As a general rule, flowers fall into 1 of 3 types of geometric form, with a 4th category for the few flowers that are neither one form nor another.

1 Mass	**2** Filler	**3** Line	**4** Structural
e.g. Allium	e.g. Gypsohilia	e.g. Gladioli	e.g. Anthurium
Dianthus	Limonium	Liatris	Strelitzia
Gerbera	Solidaster		Calla

Using several flowers of one form will give your floral design unity and harmony. Using a variety of different forms adds interest and texture.

5 PRINCIPLES AND ELEMENTS OF DESIGN

ENGLISH PRINCIPLES OF DESIGN

The English Principles of Design are as follows:

1 Balance – Actual and Visual

2 Contrast

3 Dominance

4 Harmony

5 Proportion: 2/3rds – 1/3rd

6 Rhythm

I will assume that the basic English
Principles are well understood.

EUROPEAN PRINCIPLES OF DESIGN

The Floristry Principles of Design are as follows:

The above Principles have been simplified. There are more criteria to add into most sections when working to an experienced level.

1. Overall Outline Shape	2. Initial Expression Of Style	3. Direction Of Flower Lines / Stems	4. Point of Growth (focal area) in Relation to The container	5. Amounts Of Points of Growth	6. Direction Of Growth (the visual Direction of The whole Design)	7. Techniques Included in The Construction
Symmetrical	Decorative	Radial	Above	One point	Vertical	Texturing
Asymmetrical	Form-Linear	Winding	Inside	Several equally spaced points	Horizontal	Structures
	Vegetative	Parallel	Below	Several unequally spaced points	Diagonal	Constructions
	Formal	Diagonal	Beside		Symmetrical	Layering
		Crossing				Stacking
		Free				Bundling
						Interweaving
						Winding

CREATING A FLORAL ARRANGEMENT BY USING THE FLORISTRY PRINCIPLES OF DESIGN

When starting a floral design, you would take one item from each one of the seven Principles listed on the previous page, except the very last. For example, one element from each of the following:

1 Overall outline shape - Asymmetrical

2 Initial Expression of Style - Decorative

3 Direction of the Flower lines/stems - Parallel

4 Point of Growth (focal area) - Below the container

5 Amount of points of growth - Several unequally spaced points of growth

6 Direction of growth - Vertical.

From the last of the seven Principles, 'Techniques included in Construction,' you may choose several techniques to include in your design if you wish. Just bear in mind that too many could result in overkill and you would lose effect, rather than create impact with your design. For example:

7 Techniques included in construction: - texturing

DEFINITIONS OF TERMS USING THE EUROPEAN PRINCIPLES OF DESIGN

SYMMETRICAL

The dictionary definition of 'symmetrical' is: 'having the same proportions, design, and shape on both sides.'

The floristry design definition is the same as the dictionary definition. A floristry design has equal proportions. Instead of focal lines and groups we talk of 'Dominant' or 'Principle' areas (centrally placed) and then 'Sub-dominant' or 'Secondary' areas that are placed in equal distances from the dominant group.

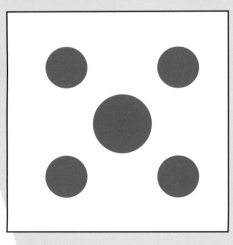

ASYMMETRICAL

The dictionary definition of 'asymmetrical' is: 'not symmetrical, lack of symmetry.'

The floristry design definition is: opposite to the symmetrical design. The Dominant/Principle group is never placed centrally, as this would make the design symmetrical - Always position this group off-centre. You will have a Sub-dominant/Secondary placement and also a smaller contrasting or Complimentary group. The groups can be linked in some way. It is important that the distances between the groups are not equal. The smallest group is always placed closest to the Principle group and therefore the Secondary group will always be positioned furthest from the Principle group.

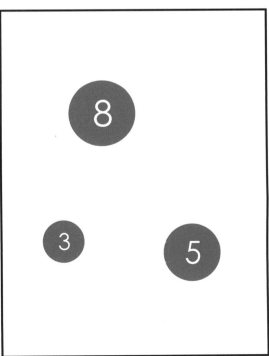

DECORATIVE

The dictionary definition of 'decorative' is: 'to make more attractive by adding something ornamental'. 'Ornamental' instead of 'functional'.

The floristry design definition is: 'the use of lots of flower materials'. The floral designer dictates and manipulates flower materials into position. There is no negative space in the design. The emphasis in the arrangement is on texture and colour. English arrangements have a tendency to be decorative, as this is generally seen as the most commercial type of design.

FORMAL

The dictionary definition of 'formal' is: 'stiff in manner, organised'

The floristry design definition is: 'often symmetrical in style. Used for a formal occasion'.

My reason for including 'Formal' within this section is this; in the U.K. we have certain items such as based sympathy tributes and compact posies that fall into this definition more easily than any other. Also, whilst the overall outline shape is formal (symmetrical) the cluster of flowers on a based tribute can be asymmetrical, symmetrical, form-linear or decorative. Lots of flower material would normally define a decorative design but the lack of space around the flowers, making it compact, makes the definition formal.

FORM LINEAR

The dictionary definition of 'form-linear' is: 'orderly method of arrangement, manner of co-ordinating elements, e.g. in the presentation of ideas. 'the structural plan, element of a design or work of art.' 'characterised by an emphasis on line having clearly defined outlines.'

The floristry design definition is: 'there is an emphasis on line, form and movement'. Negative space is very important in this arrangement. The flower material forms dictate the position and use to the floral designer. This is often a limited flower design and can look quite structural and contemporary. The point of growth is often below or inside the container, with the direction of the stems being radial.

VEGETATIVE

The dictionary definition of 'vegetative' is: 'of or like plants or vegetables'.

The floristry design definition is: 'Nature dictates the style and placement of flower materials to the designer'. It is important to interpret nature rather than copy nature.

Your arrangement will have a theme but will not look like a scene. For example, when using sand, rocks, water, grasses – do not create a pretty picture but make your design an interpretation of a beach theme. Use your imagination. Your choice of materials should be from the same natural habitat and your container as natural as possible. Have respect for the stages of growth of your flowers. Although in 'normal' floristry we use the larger, more open flowers near the focal area and the buds towards the outlines, in Vegetative designs we must use the flowers as they would naturally grow. Therefore, the buds are at the shortest point and the more open, mature flowers will be the tallest ones.

A vegetative design will normally have asymmetrical points of growth – several unequally spaced groups with radial focal points of growth.

RADIAL

The dictionary definition of 'radial' is: 'arranged like rays, radiating from a central point or axis.' 'Characterised by divergence from a central point.'

The floristry design definition is: the flowers can be in lines like rays, radiating from a central point. Alternatively these may be groups, still with the stems radiating from a central point.

PARALLEL

The dictionary definition of 'parallel' is: 'side by side, having the same distance continuously between them'.

The floristry design definition is: the flowers are placed equidistant to each other. The stems will also be equidistantly placed. The point of growth will be either below or in the container. There is often low spreading material based in-between the groups. As well as the positions of the flower material you must pay attention to the visual and actual texture of the design. However, there can be several groupings of flowers that could be either evenly or unevenly positioned. So the stem placement, even though equidistant could be in asymmetrical or symmetrical groups.

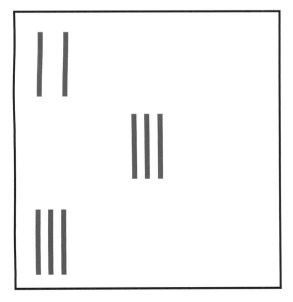

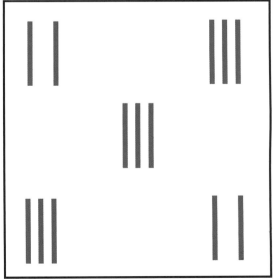

WINDING

The dictionary definition of 'winding' is: 'wound or coiled around about an object. A curved line, course or progress.'

The floristry design definition is: the same as the dictionary one and is self evident. There could also be several (probably unevenly spaced) growth points. This is a more natural effect and is not often used as a decorative technique.

DIAGONAL

The dictionary definition of 'diagonal' is: 'running in an oblique line from the vertical, crossways, slanting.'

The floristry design definition is: 'the above definition has the same points of order'. There can also be several points of growth. Stem placement can be random or equidistant.

CROSSING

The dictionary definition of 'crossing' is: 'traversing or travelling across. 'Place where one thing crosses another.'

The floristry design definition is: 'stems can cross with each other in a mix of parallel and diagonal styles'. This style can emphasise structured arrangement, so the use of a little foliage and bare stems will look more effective.

FREE

The dictionary definition of 'free' is: 'voluntary, spontaneous, not hampered or restricted.'

The floristry design definition is: 'whilst this arrangement looks random, it is anything but, and requires knowledge and skill in order to create harmony'. It can have several points of growth.

VERTICAL

The dictionary definition of 'vertical' is: 'perpendicular to the plane of the horizon, or to a primary axis'.

The floristry design definition is: 'the proportions of your arrangement would be taller than its width or depth'.

HORIZONTAL

The dictionary definition of 'horizontal' is: 'parallel to the horizon or a base line'.

The floristry design definition is: 'the proportions of your arrangement would be wider than the height or depth'.

TEXTURING

The dictionary definition of 'texturing' is: 'the visual or tactile surface characteristics of something.'

The floristry design definition is: very similar to the dictionary definition in that we use the visual or actual surface texture of flower materials to create interest within the design. Regardless of whether they are fluffy, feathery, silky, velvety or waxy, be aware of the effects of using too many textures in one design.

LAYERING

The dictionary definition of 'layering' is: 'to set in order or position. A single thickness, lying over or under another as part of a series.'

The floristry design definition is: the same as the dictionary one. Layering is a technique where materials are placed low down in the design. Not specifically one type of material. There is no space in between and can have a scale-like appearance.

INTERWEAVING

The dictionary definition of 'interweaving' is: 'to intermingle, blend. 'To weave together.'

The floristry design definition is: 'to weave materials together', typically leaves or other materials, into a decorative style. You may use woven items as an integral design feature in all manner of arrangements, from sympathy tributes to pedestal designs.

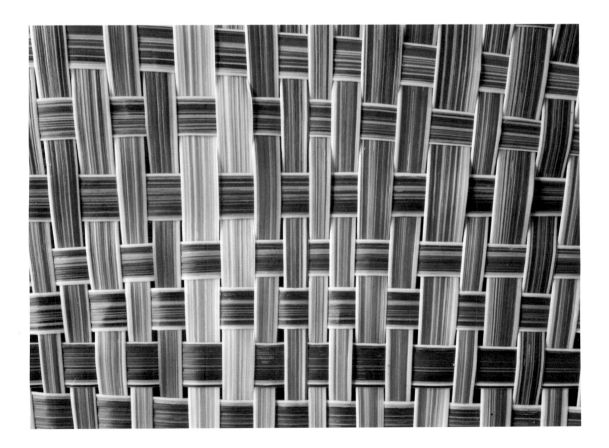

CONSTRUCTION AND STRUCTURE

The dictionary definition of 'construction' is 'to build or put together. 'The process, art or manner of constructing.'

The dictionary definition of structure is: 'something that is constructed, organised in a definite pattern.'

With regard to the floristry design definition of these terms, there is often confusion as to whether the frameworks we make from wire and twigs etc. are structures or constructions. These frameworks are often decorative and/or are built to support flower materials.

One way to define the difference between the two when deciding which to use in our designs is this: if the majority of the framework is visible, and its visibility is integral to the design, and if the flowers only cover a part of the design, then this is a CONSTRUCTION. If the majority of the framework is covered by flowers and is being used mainly as a supporting mechanic, then it has become a STRUCTURE.

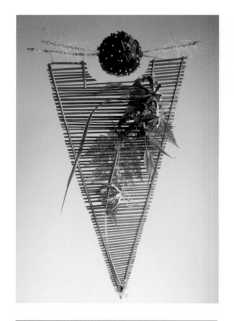

STACKING

The dictionary definition of 'stacking' is: 'an orderly pile or heap.'

The floristry design definition is: 'flower materials of a similar shape and size placed next to one another'. These are often very flat materials. They may be used as an individual form in itself and placed as part of the design, for example, a 'kebab-style' stick stacked with Lunaria discs.

BUNDLING

The dictionary definition of 'bundling' is: 'a collection of things held together, mostly parallel.'

The floristry design definition is: 'several materials (normally the same type) tied together and either used as the whole design, for example, a Wheat sheaf'. Or small amounts, such as short Cornus stem bundles tied with bullion wire and used decoratively as part of the design.

7

FOCAL AREAS – POINTS OF GROWTH

In this Chapter, we consider what would have been called the 'Focal Area' in traditional English Design. Within the European Design Principles these Focal Areas are termed ' Points of Growth', but there is a distinct and important difference

THE NUMBER OF POINTS OF GROWTH

Within the Floristry Design Principles there are several options for the number of points of growth within designs. In simplistic terms these are:

Single point

Several equally spaced points

Several points unequally/randomly spaced

Single Points of Growth: One grouping of flowers where all stems appear to start from the same point. This radial placement of stems is reflective of nature. Many plants, such as ferns, grow in this manner and therefore are suitable for use in a vegetative style arrangement.

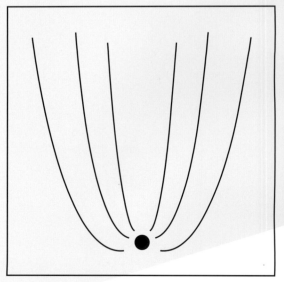

Several Points of Growth: Asymmetrical arrangements will have several points of growth. They will not be equally spaced and point of growth is often radial. In contrast, parallel arrangements are symmetrical and will have equally spaced points of growth.

Several uneven points of growth

Several even points of growth

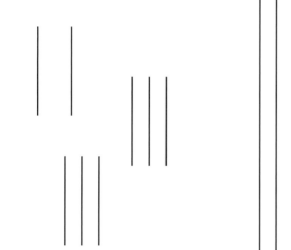
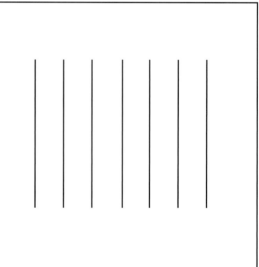

POINT OF GROWTH IN RELATION TO THE CONTAINER

The focal area of a European Design is slightly different than in a 'British' arrangement. A British design would have a very visible focal area, usually defined by a floral focal line/flower from which all other flowers/lines and groups seem to radiate. Such a traditional design would consider the flower as the focal area and the stem placement is irrelevant, as it is very rarely visible as part of the design.

These new principles look at the point at which the stems start as the focal area and stem placement is very important. It is referred to as a 'point of growth', rather than a focal area, and may be visible or implied. The design still evolves from this point and the eye will naturally flow to and from that point if the design has harmony.

For example; in a British symmetrical arrangement, the focal area, the point through which all flowers flow through, is normally a flower line/flower or group and the container is often concealed. In European designs, the point of growth can be invisible or implied. The point where the 'eye' flows to or from can be inside, outside, beside, or below the container. That is why it is very important to position the stems very carefully and deliberately as the eye follows through to the point at which they converge. This is the Point of Growth.

There are four possible placements for your point of growth, given in the examples below:

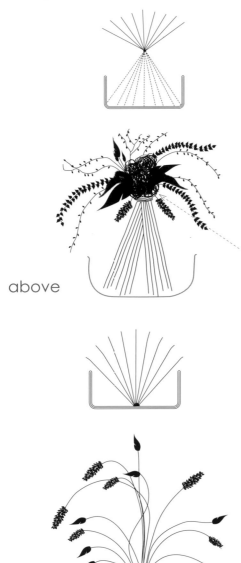

above

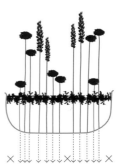

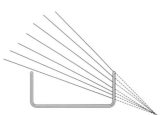

below

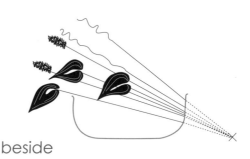

inside

beside

FORMAL DESIGN VERSUS DECORATIVE DESIGN

Formal or Decorative? That is the question....?

Every design you make has the ability to become either a Formal or a Decorative piece. Formal designs are often more limited in style and flower material and Decorative designs are plentiful in techniques and flower material.

There is a sliding scale along which there is an accepted degree of variance. The problem arises when neither of the styles dominates and you cannot tell whether a design is Formal or Decorative.

So, as a general rule of thumb, go easy when choosing the techniques from the last row of the Principles of Design provided in the previous Chapter if you want a more formal/compact arrangement, such as a biedermeier. Alternatively, you may take a free hand with the flowers and foliage if you want a more Decorative style.

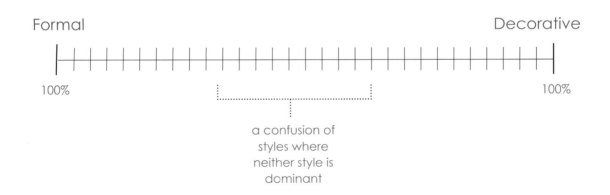

Formal   Decorative

100%   100%

a confusion of
styles where
neither style is
dominant

8 THE ELEMENTS OF DESIGN

English Elements of Design

The English Elements of Design are listed below and I have made the assumption that the reader will be familiar with these.

Colour

Form

Space

Texture

European Elements of Design

The European Elements of Design are very similar to the English but you can see from the list below that the principle difference is the addition of 'Movement'.

Form

Movement/Lines

Texture

Colour

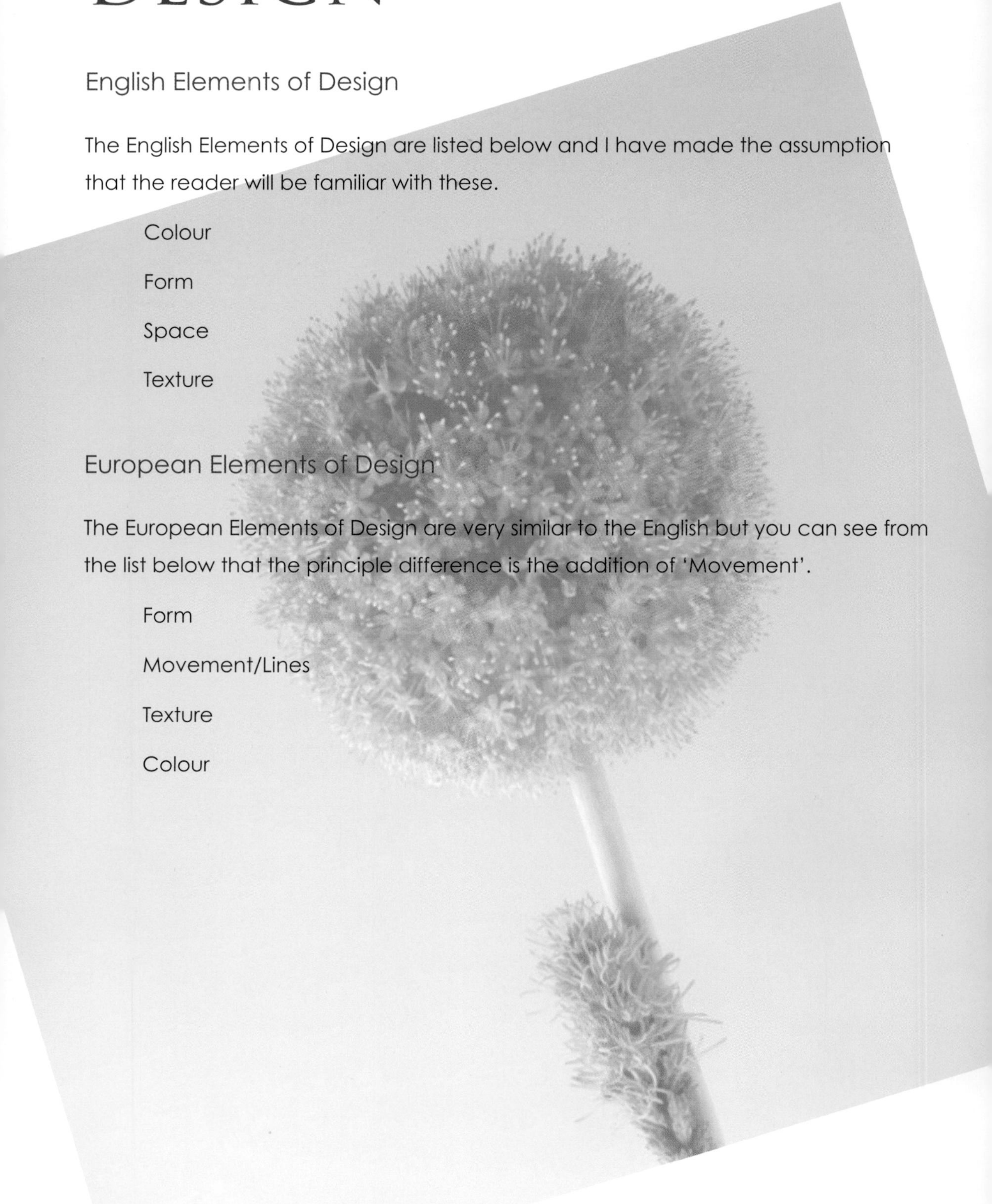

FORM

The dictionary definition for 'form' is: 'shape or appearance, type or kind'.

In the floristry design definition there are two types of form. These are 'Natural' and 'Created'.

Natural Forms are items such as trees, foliage, flowers, animals and some types of containers. In Natural Forms you will rarely find completely straight lines or 90-degree angles. No two items will be entirely identical.

Created Forms are, as their title suggests, man-made and, because of this, they may be full of straight lines and 90-degree angles. They are able to be reproduced identically.

See also the Section under Visual Impact of Flowers in Chapter 4 to relate form to the visual outline shape.

MOVEMENT/LINES

The dictionary definition of 'movement/lines' is: 'change in position or place, action or process of moving'.

The floristry design definition is: 'recognises that each flower material has its own natural movement and direction of growth that must be respected when they are used within designs'. It is important not to cut flowers short, using a little stem or just the head of the flower. The stem indicates the movement of the flower and it is important to show the whole stem.

Flower Movement may be translated as 'Growth Direction'

UPWARDS

Always give these tall spike-like flowers space to grow/open. Do not position them is such a way that the flower placed above it 'blocks' the movement.

Angled
Eucharis with one head open

Angled
Eucharis with several heads open.

Flowers change their movement by opening out. Remember to allow for this possibility when designing your arrangement.

Hanging/trailing
Amaranthus

Curving
gentle flowing curves – Crocosmia

Upwards and unfolding
Helianthus, moves strongly upwards then unfolds into a round resting head.

There are also other materials we may use in floristry such as recessive or resting materials. They can be man-made or natural items. Do not cover this movement with a larger material, for example, a large leaf.

Meandering

playful curves gently moving, for example – Gloriosa.

Resting

flat or low growing – Semperviens

Spreading

normally low growing materials such as moss.

Tortured/bizarre

materials with lots of thorns. Do not place large materials in front or on top of this growth pattern. It needs space and freedom to move.

TEXTURE

The dictionary definition of 'texture' is: 'structure, feel or consistency'.

The floristry design definition is: 'the florist considers texture in two ways, firstly the actual texture – how the material feels; secondly the visual texture – how the material looks'. Texture, along with colour, portrays emotions and can create atmosphere. Textured materials should be used with thought and placed with care in any design.

Texture, both visual and actual, is also to be applied within the proportions of Phi – 3:5:8. Examples of texture are shown below.

COLOUR

The dictionary definition of 'colour' is: 'appearance of things as a result of reflecting light'.

The floristry design definition is: There are several variations on how best to create and explain the colour wheel that have been devised over the years by many people. However, the end result is always the same. There are twelve colours of varying tint, tone, shade and hue that can be achieved through colour modification by use of achromatic colours.

A Little Background information.

Pigments have been used almost since the beginning of time to 'colour' drawings and fabrics. The first colour wheel as we know it was devised by Sir Isaac Newton in 1706. He took the white sunlight beams and split them into red, orange, yellow, green, cyan and blue beams. He then joined the 2 ends of the spectrum into a circle to show natural colour progression.

Approximately 100 years later around 1810 Johann Wolfgang Goethe studied the psychological effect of colours and realised that colours are also shaped by our own personal perception.

Current colour theory is based on previous knowledge but developed by a Swiss man named Johannes Itten. In the mid 1900's he modified the colour wheels in use. It is this man that we have to thank for our understanding of colour and colour wheels. They are now based on the primary colours, red, yellow and blue and then developed into 12 hues. Johannes Itten wrote a groundbreaking book on colour called "The Art of Colour".

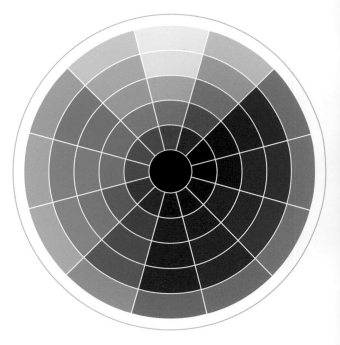

Greyscale / Achromatic

Achromatic colours are neutral colours or 'non-colours', for instance, black or white. The mixing of these will create 'greyscale'. When any part of the greyscale is added to the hue of any colour, variation in tint, tone and shade is the result.

The 'warm colours' are the advancing colours, such as red, orange and yellow. The 'cool colours' are the receding or recessive colours, such as blue, green and violet. Both types of colour are emotive, either exciting or calming the symbolism of the design, depending on their tonal value.

Advancing / warm

Receding / cool

HOW TO USE COLOUR
IN FLORAL DESIGNS

Colour is emotive. Colour choices within any design are often subconsciously influenced by the designer's past and culture. Colour preferences can have influence and even dominance over an entire design. Colour can, if used without proper care, take precedence over the form of the flower used, but in any design form should normally retain dominance.

It is most important that a designer considers the visual balance (weight/influence) of a colour within the 3:5:8 proportions. Form and colour value should be harmoniously balanced to create exciting floral designs.

HOW TO USE THE PRINCIPLES AND ELEMENTS OF DESIGN

Use the Principles of Design chart on page 30 to help you examine and understand the following photographs.

1 Symmetrical

2 Formal

3 Parallel

4 Inside the container

5 Several evenly spaced points of growth

6 Symmetrical

7 Texturing and construction

1 Symmetrical

2 Decorative

3 Parallel

4 Inside the container

5 Several unevenly spaced points of growth

6 Horizontal

7 Texturing and winding

1 Asymmetrical

2 Vegetative

3 Radial

4 Below

5 Several
unevenly
spaced points
of growth

6 Vertical

7 Texture

1 Symmetrical

2 Decorative

3 Radial

4 Above the container

5 One point of growth

6 Symmetrical

7 Structure, winding, bundling, texturing.

1 Asymmetrical

2 Decorative

3 Crossing

4 Inside

5 Several Unevenly
spaced

6 Horizontal

7 Texturing/stacking

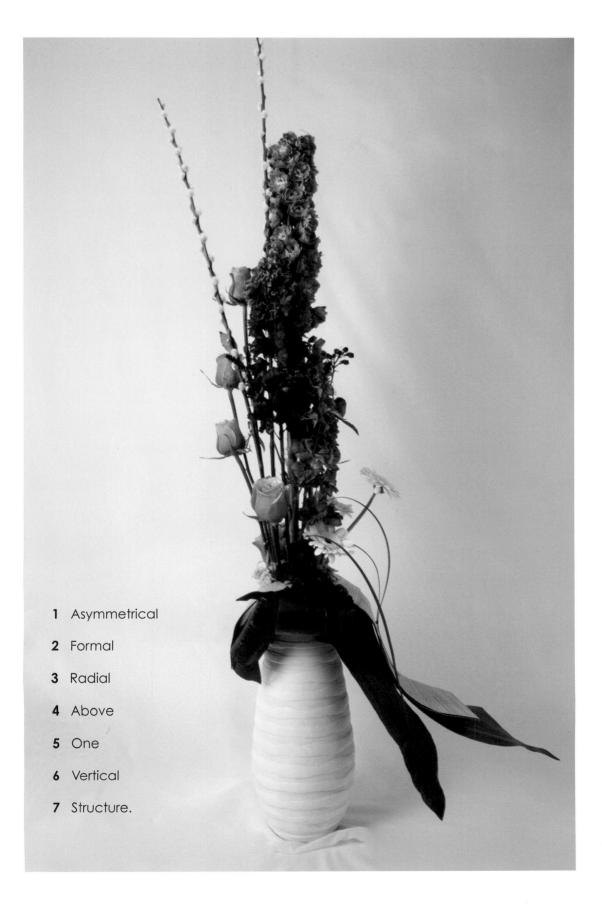

1 Asymmetrical

2 Formal

3 Radial

4 Above

5 One

6 Vertical

7 Structure.

1 Asymmetrical

2 Formal

3 Diagonal

4 Beside

5 Several unevenly spaced

6 Diagonal

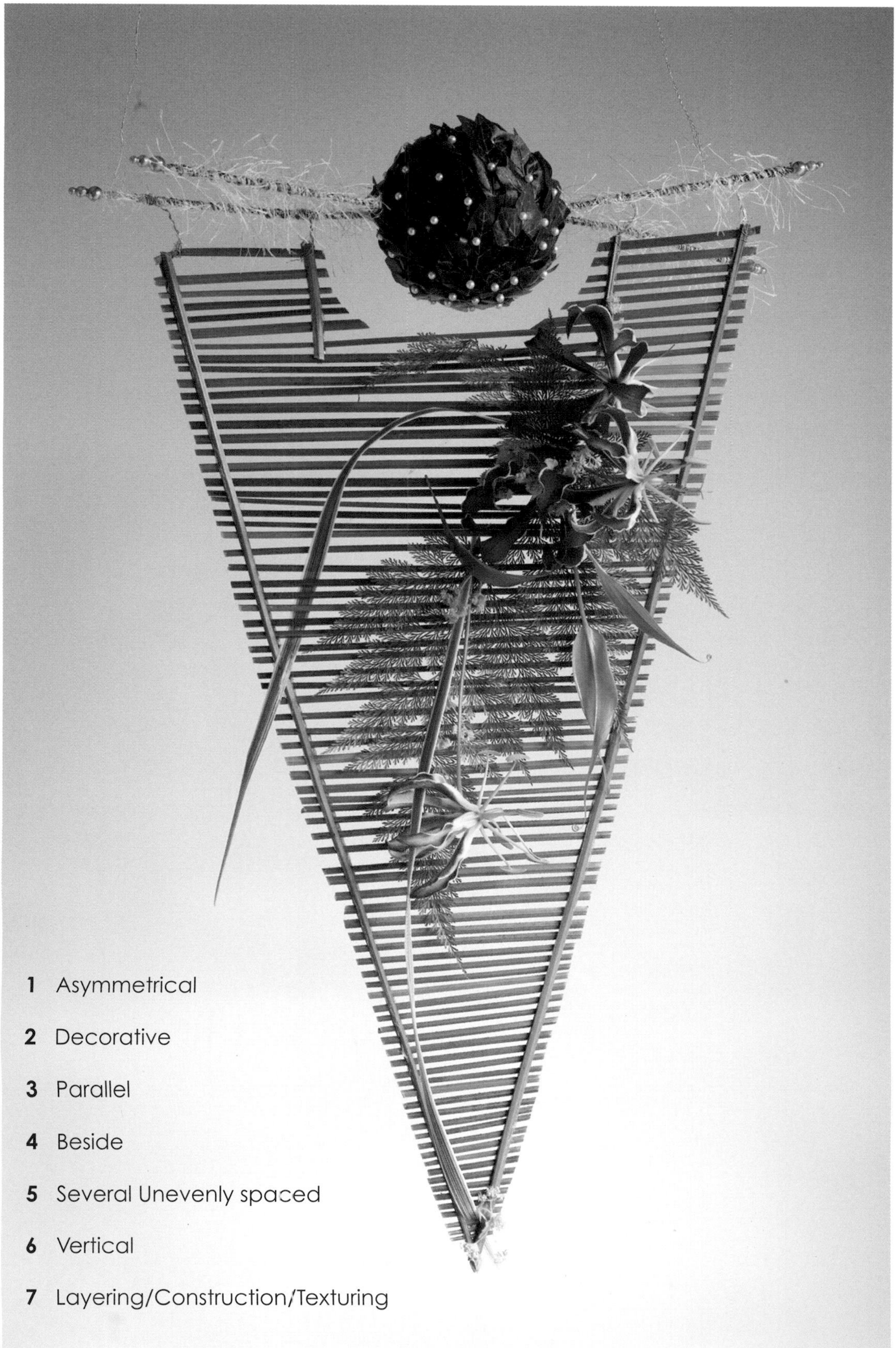

1 Asymmetrical

2 Decorative

3 Parallel

4 Beside

5 Several Unevenly spaced

6 Vertical

7 Layering/Construction/Texturing

WHERE DOES OUR INSPIRATION COME FROM?

Every country using these Floristry Principles of Design has their own style. The end results may occasionally look similar but there will be subtle differences. The differences result from the way in which each culture adapts the principles, in order to fit their own requirements and design or even retail customs. Although we are currently inspired by Europe and its design trends, we need to understand and adopt the relevant design principles - not necessarily the design style.

Ultimately, there is no right or wrong flower placement. If the flower position or design style is where the designer wishes it to be and he has followed the initial principle of design guidelines, then he can have complete confidence in the work that has been done.

Just as each country develops their own style, so will each florist or designer from that country develop their own 'signature' style within the boundaries of the Principles and Elements of Design.

Once you have understood these simplified and basic principles of design and you have been putting them into practice. There are other elements to begin to consider within each category. For example, when creating a vegetative design you will have three other options – a vegetative parallel, a decorative vegetative and a graphic vegetative.

So how do we, as British florists, develop our own style? There is no simple answer or magic method that can be applied. Each florist must look inside and create from within, from the heart.

Examine your past, your present and your future. Take a close look at your childhood, your upbringing and your culture. What is your nationality? Examine carefully the influences on you today - emotions, hobbies, architecture, art etc. From these will come your own unique design inspiration.

What about your future? Think about current and possible future trends and also where you wish to be in a few years time. Look at your existing knowledge and understanding of floristry and also your general knowledge. All these will help shape and energise your design abilities.

Lastly, your passion, drive and enthusiasm for our industry will inspire you. The flowers, and plants themselves, their colours, textures and scents, will influence your designs. Remember, the sources of inspiration are personal to you alone. Therefore, the arranging style that you achieve is also yours alone.

Above all, have confidence in your ability and understanding.

Allow yourself to be inspired.

Enjoy yourself and have fun!